ANTHROPOLOGICAL PAPERS
MUSEUM OF ANTHROPOLOGY, UNIVERSITY OF MICHIGAN
No. 3

Cave Hollow, An Ozark Bluff – Dweller Site

by
HORACE MINER

ANN ARBOR
UNIVERSITY OF MICHIGAN PRESS, 1950

ISBN (print): 978-1-949098-40-2
ISBN (ebook): 978-1-951519-64-3

Browse all of our books at sites.lsa.umich.edu/archaeology-books.

Order our books from the University of Michigan Press at www.press.umich.edu.

For permissions, questions, or manuscript queries, contact Museum publications by email at ummapubs@umich.edu or visit the Museum website at lsa.umich.edu/ummaa.

CONTENTS

CAVE HOLLOW, AN OZARK BLUFF-DWELLER SITE[1]

INTRODUCTION

Cave Hollow is situated in north-central Arkansas, fifteen miles south of the Missouri state line and 6.6 miles northeast of Pyatt on the Blue Heaven Road (Yellville Quad; sec. 22, T. 19 N., R. 17 W.). The ravine in which the cave is situated is part of the drainage system of the White River. The passages of the cave are just extended enough to permit human entrance, but the cave mouth expands to provide a large open shelter below the cliff face, near the rim of the ravine (Fig. 1). The southern exposure of the entrance added to its desirability for human occupancy. The floor of the entrance is partly covered with large rocks which have fallen from the roof, particularly near the mouth. Under and around the rocks there was formerly an accumulation of sand and ashes several feet thick. These deposits were limited to the floor of the entrance to the cave.

When I first saw the site, the ash bed was exposed and intact only in the northwestern corner of the cave mouth, behind the rockfall visible in Figure 1. The rest of the deposit had been excavated by a field party from the University of Arkansas in the summer of 1948. A long interest in archaeology and the limited extent of the undisturbed deposit led me to undertake the excavation of the remaining ash bed during a short stay in the vicinity in April, 1949. Full report on this site awaits publication by the University of Arkansas. As this has not yet appeared and as there is a paucity of material on specific Ozark Bluff-Dweller sites, it seems wise to present the results of the less extensive excavation.

[1]I am indebted to Dr. James B. Griffin for his assistance in the preparation of this report and for extending to me the facilities of the Ceramic Repository of the Museum of Anthropology, University of Michigan. Mr. Martin, who operates the farm on which the site is located, kindly consented to the excavation. I also gratefully acknowledge the field assistance of Miss Denise Miner.

Figure 1

STRUCTURE OF THE DEPOSIT

The area excavated fell within a 5-foot horizontal grid. Within this area the sandy ash deposit varied in depth from zero, where the cave floor rose to become the cave wall, to 33 inches at its deepest point. The top of the deposit lay 2 to 3.5 feet below the cave roof, sloping downward toward the center and toward the mouth of the cave. The cave is damp, and the top 4 to 5 inches of the ash bed were partly solidified by minerals deposited by the drip from the roof. Artifacts at all levels had similar lime deposits, probably from seepage. Bone material, however, was well preserved. There was no trace of the vegetal material characteristic of dry shelters in the Ozarks.[2] It is noteworthy that there was no evidence of lime-hardened levels within the deposit itself. This would seem to argue that the deposits accumulated over a fairly continuous period of habitation, after which the surface crust had an opportunity to form.

Three crude hearths were situated in crevices and between rocks on the floor of the cave. The construction of the hearths was so simple that only evidences of fire—ash concentration, burned bones, and stones—indicated their use. Artifacts were more concentrated in and near the hearths. The stone artifacts at the floor level were unbroken or reworked broken pieces. In the deposit which covered the floor and hearth level, artifacts consisted largely of broken fragments. Flint chips and animal bones occurred throughout the deposit. All long bones had been split open, presumably to obtain the marrow.

A reconstruction of the use of the back corner of the cave mouth makes it evident that it first served for living purposes. Cooking was done between rocks on the cave floor. Spears, or their points, and scrapers and knives were left near these centers of domestic activity. Later, the activities were transferred elsewhere in the cave mouth and refuse was thrown into this then unused part of the cave. As the midden accumulated the diminishing space between it and the cave roof made the area impractical for further cooking activities.

ECONOMY AND BONE ARTIFACTS

Materials in the midden indicate that the following animals were used for food: mussels, box terrapin, turkey, fox squirrel, opossum, raccoon, gray fox, and deer.[3] No evidence of

[2] M. R. Harrington, "The Ozark Bluff-Dwellers," Amer. Anthropol., XXVI (1924): 1-21.

[3] I am indebted to Dr. William Burt, of the Museum of Zoology, University of Michigan, for identification of the mammalian material.

agriculture was found, although other sites show that it was practiced by the Ozark Bluff Dwellers.

Two whole dorsal parts of box terrapin carapace were in the midden in addition to fragments and scattered ventral portions. They bore no signs of having been cut or otherwise shaped. Fragments of two bone awls were formed from split and ground metatarsal and metacarpal bones of deer.

POTTERY

Only eight sherds were found, but they provide evidence of stratigraphy. Two ceramic types are represented. One type is of a crude ware which was tempered with burned clay particles. Sherds of this type range in thickness from 8 to 13 mm. The surface is crudely smoothed and is light brown, clouded with gray. The interior paste and surface are black. Sufficient material was recovered to determine that the sherds were from a cylindrical type of vessel. The only curvature evidenced was that of the circumference. One reconstructed section was from a vessel 163 mm. in diameter. The base type is flat without textile marking. No rim sherds were found.

This pottery is typical of the Ozark Bluff Dwellers. It has been found with Marksville and Coles Creek wares,[4] but the plain wares which are associated with Marksville, Troyville, and Coles Creek pottery outside of Louisiana are so similar that Phillips, Griffin, and Ford identify this general type as Baytown Plain.[5] Pottery appears in the later part of Ozark Bluff-Dweller occupations, but has occurred as deep as 37 inches.[6] Sherds of this type at Cave Hollow were 3 to 20 inches below the surface, the deepest being associated with a hearth. No prepottery occupation is indicated.

The other type of pottery at Cave Hollow is represented by three sherds found at depths of 5 to 10 inches. This ware is thin (4.5 to 6 mm.) and shell-tempered. The sherds are from globular vessels. The surfaces are roughly smoothed, and

[4]S. C. Dellinger and S. D. Dickinson, "Pottery from the Ozark Bluff Shelters," Amer. Antiq., VII (1941-42): 276-89.

[5]In their forthcoming survey of the Mississippi Valley, to be published by the Peabody Museum.

[6]Dellinger and Dickinson, *op. cit.*, p. 277.

the surface and paste is gray to black. The ware is a Mississippi type. Harrington[7] stated that a shell-tempered ware is found on the surface of Bluff-Dweller sites and attributes this "Top Layer" culture to a later people than the Bluff Dwellers. The evidence from Cave Hollow is consistent with this interpretation as the Bluff-Dweller pottery occurs at lower levels than the Mississippi ware. The two wares were mixed, however, in the top 10 inches of the cave deposit. As both types appear below the lime-caked crust which tops the deposit, no long time interval between them is indicated. Their co-occurrence in the top levels of the midden does not necessarily mean contemporaneity. Older materials may have been scraped up with more recent refuse in the formation of the midden. The evidence certainly does not preclude contact between the two cultures.

STONE ARTIFACTS

Thirty-three chipped stone artifacts were excavated. The material in most instances is flint, but five pieces are of quartzite. The flint varies greatly in color—white, cream, pink, olive, various shades of gray, and browns from caramel to wine. Most are of fairly homogeneous color, although some of the gray flint is banded with lighter or darker gray. One blade fragment is of very distinctive flint, a mottled gray, black, and red-brown. All of the flint, to judge from the irregularity of the flake scars, is of relatively poor quality. Some of the material is clearly chert.

Artifacts consist of the whole or part of fifteen projectile points, eleven blades, six ovoid scrapers, and one "thumbnail" scraper. Flint flakes were found in small numbers in the midden. One of these flakes is drill-shaped, having a protrusion 2 cm. long, the last half of which is 7 mm. wide. There is no secondary chipping, but the worn edge of the protrusion indicates that the flake was used as a drill. A hammerstone of nodular flint provides evidence of the use of unworked stone. There were no artifacts of ground stone.

Eight different types of projectile points were collected. All were double convex in cross section. Points from the

[7] *Op. cit.*, p. 12.

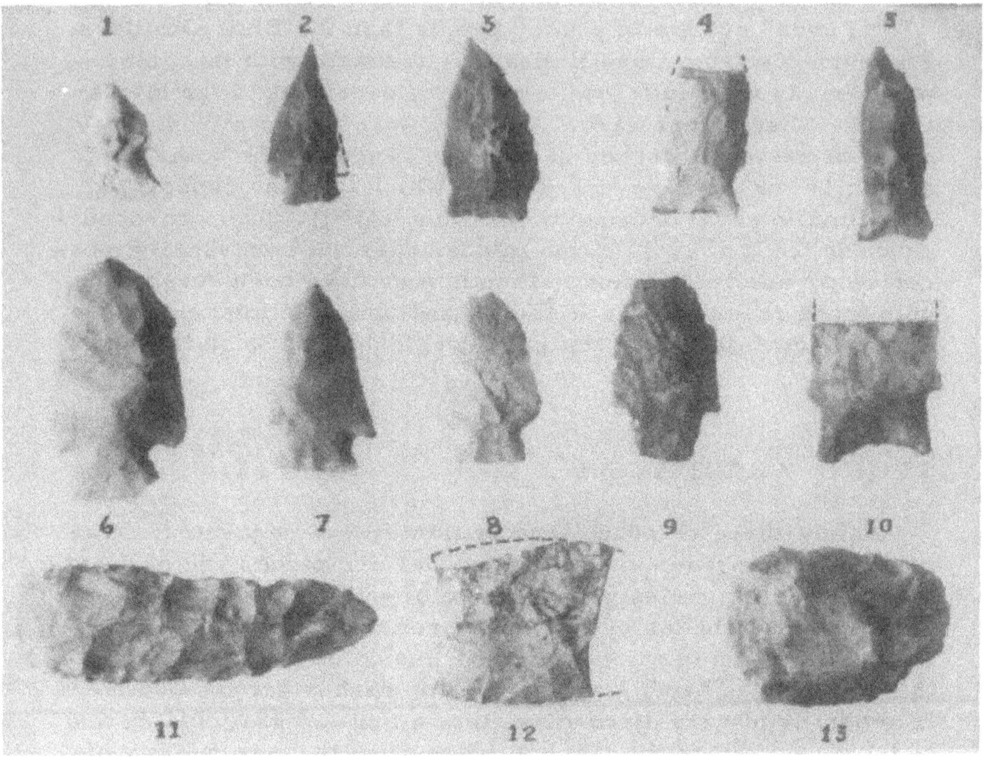

Figure 2

floor level of the cave have contracting stems[8] (Fig. 2, Nos. 1, 6-8) with the exception of one piece with an expanding stem (Fig. 2, No. 9). The points with contracting stems are all over 55 mm. in length (maximum 78 mm.) except one, which is 37 mm. long (Fig. 2, No. 1). This point is also distinctive in that it has a convex base; the others have straight bases. The stem of the small point makes up half its length, in contrast to the medium length of the stems of the other points. The eight

[8]Contracting from the base. This terminology follows Fay-Cooper Cole and Thorne Deuel, Rediscovering Illinois (Chicago, 1937), p. 286.

points with contrasting stems are barbed[9] or have straight or receding shoulders. The same point may have two shoulder types (Fig. 2, No. 7). The aim in manufacture seems to have been a barbed point. The four of these points made of better flint are all barbed. Of the four unbarbed points, two are of quartzite, including the mixed type noted above, another is of chert, and another of a flint with very poor flaking properties.

Three of the points with contracting stems had been broken and reworked. A new point had been made on one, and another had been worked into a convex scraper at its distal end. An attempt to convert the third broken point into a scraper had apparently been abandoned.

Three other types of stemmed points were found in the midden. The basal parts of two straight-stemmed, concave-based points indicate one type (Fig. 2, No. 10). To judge by the width (43 mm.) and the parallel sides of the blade, this was probably a relatively long point. The small lateral projection where the blade and shoulder join is noteworthy. There is a straight-stemmed, straight-based, square-shouldered point, 52 mm. long (Fig. 2, No. 2). Another point is apparently intentionally asymmetrical and has a poorly defined stem with sloping shoulders (Fig. 2, No. 3).

Two points are unstemmed. One is straight-based and has shallow side notches (Fig. 2, No. 4). The other is slender and has a concave flared base, and the sides of the blade contract from the base and then expand slightly before narrowing to the point (Fig. 2, No. 5).

Long pointed blades were the next most numerous type of stone artifact. Fragments of nine were found in the deposit at depths of 2.5 to 18 inches. The only complete blade, which was found on the cave floor under 23 inches of midden, is 112 mm. long and has a maximum width of 35 mm. (Fig. 2, No. 11). The shortest blade seems to have been about 8 cm. long. Widths vary from 29 to 43 mm. The basal ends are straight or convex. A fragment of a distinctively wider blade (50 mm.) with a concave base was uncovered at a depth of 10 inches (Fig. 2, No. 12). It was no thicker in cross section (11 mm.) than the narrower pieces.

Ovoid scrapers (Fig. 2, No. 13) vary from 50 to 70 mm. in length and from 6 to 17 mm. in thickness. Half of them had

[9]The combination of contracting stem and barb is sometimes referred to as "corner-notched."

been made by reworking one side of a large flake. The others have secondary chipping on both faces. Both types of scrapers occurred at all levels of the excavation. A single "thumbnail" scraper is 32 mm. long, with secondary flaking on both surfaces. The distal end and the sides are edged and straight. They meet at right angles. The proximal end is blunt and convex.

Most of the types of stone artifacts are represented by a single specimen. Under the circumstances any conclusions as to stratigraphy have a large possible error, but it is significant that all of the points with contracting stems were found at the bottom of the midden. The only other stone artifacts that occurred in numbers were blades and ovoid scrapers. Both were present at all levels of the site. As Mississippi-type points were absent, the pottery sequence is not duplicated in the flint material.

STONEWORK COMPARISONS

The stone artifact types from Cave Hollow will be identified in the following discussion by the numbers of the specimens illustrated in Figure 2. In spite of the attention devoted to Ozark Bluff-Dweller vegetal materials and pottery, the stonework has been virtually undescribed. Harrington stated that the most characteristic spear head is "diamond shape, with more or less pointed base."[10] He added that side-notched and stemmed forms frequently occurred and that there were also "rude flint scrapers." Some of his illustrations show heavy ovoid ax blades, not duplicated at Cave Hollow. In one plate Harrington pictured the remains of hafted spearheads. Of these, the one complete point is short and triangular with a stem, the nature of which cannot be ascertained from the figure.

Walker illustrated points excavated from Cedar Grove Cave, near Gilbert, Arkansas, in the same general area as Cave Hollow.[11] The projectile-point series from the two

[10] Op. cit., p. 5.

[11] Winslow M. Walker, "The Cave Culture of Arkansas," Explorations and Field-Work of the Smithsonian Institution in 1931 (Washington, 1932), pp. 159-68.

sites is markedly similar. In Walker's Figure 156 are the Cave Hollow types Nos. 2, 3, 4, 6, 7, 8, and 9; only Nos. 1, 5, and 10 are not represented. He noted also a "crude workmanship owing partly to poor quality of flint."[12] "Knives" and "scrapers" were found at the site, but their form is not discussed. Another type of projectile point, with expanding stem, slightly defined shoulders, and pointed or rounded base, appears in Walker's illustrations. These best fit the "diamond shape" designation of Harrington and may well be an earlier form than is the straight-based type (No. 9). Associated artifacts resembling those from Cave Hollow were bone awls and "crude, undecorated, flat bottomed, shell tempered pottery."[13] The tempering at Cave Hollow was, of course, different in the equivalent type of pottery.

Because of the proximity of Cave Hollow to Missouri it is advisable to make comparisons with Woodland materials from that state. Existence of Bluff-Dweller sites is recognized in Missouri, but they apparently have not been described,[14] so that the comparison must be made with other possibly related materials.

Point type No. 1 is associated with the Highland Aspect, a late Woodland manifestation,[15] but it also occurred at Bone Cave, which only comes up through the middle Woodland period.[16] Type No. 4 was also present in Bone Cave[17] and appears in the Boone Focus, which Chapman believed to parallel the pottery horizon of the Ozark Bluff Dwellers. He considered

[12]Ibid., p. 164.

[13]Ibid., p. 162.

[14]Carl H. Chapman, "Woodland Cultures and the Ozark Bluff Dwellers," Missouri Archaeol., X (1948), Pt. 3: 95-132.

[15]Ibid., p. 100 and Fig. 24. See also Chapman's "Ancient Cultures and Sequence," Missouri Archaeol., X, Pt. 4: 155. Robert McC. Adams found this type only in the upper level of the Hidden Valley Rock Shelter, see "Archaeological Investigations in Jefferson County, Missouri 1939-40," Trans. Acad. Sci. St. Louis, XXX, No. 5 (1944): 188-96.

J. Allen Eichenberger also reported this type (his type I) as occurring in later Woodland sites: "Investigations of the Marion-Ralls Archaeological Society in Northeast Missouri," Missouri Archaeol., No. 19 (1944): 65, Pl. I.

[16]E. Adamson Hoebel, "The Archaeology of Bone Cave, Miller County, Missouri," Anthropol. Papers Amer. Mus. Nat. Hist., XL, Pt. 2 (1946): Pl. 14, Specimen A.

[17]Ibid., Pl. 14, Specimen J.

it early Woodland, but conceded that Griffin may be right in bringing it through the middle Woodland period.[18]

Point type No. 6 is Hopewellian in shape,[19] but comparatively crudely chipped. Points similar to No. 6 were found in Bone Cave as were others like No. 9.[20] Eichenberger attributed the latter type to later Woodland sites, but he associated point types Nos. 6 and 10 with earlier Woodland.[21] The long blade and concave base of No. 10 are characteristics generally associated with old horizons. The stem and shoulder features of No. 10, however, are specializations away from the Fulsom and Yuma form. These features do occur in the 9-foot preceramic "Deep Deposit" of the Lawrence site near Hot Springs, in which types Nos. 2, 4, and 11 are also present.[22]

From the Missouri comparisons we conclude that there is evidence that projectile-point types Nos. 1 and 9 occur at least from middle through late Woodland; Nos. 4 and 6 in early and middle Woodland; and No. 10 in early Woodland.[23] If Cave Hollow were placed as contemporaneous with the latter part of the middle Woodland period in Missouri there would be conformity except for the type No. 10 points. There were two specimens of this type at Cave Hollow in the midden above types Nos. 1, 6, and 9 which occurred at floor level. Possibly the two points had been scraped up with refuse from older deposits in the cave, or points of type No. 10 may have persisted longer than the early ceramic period.

If one goes farther afield than Missouri in search for

[18]Missouri Archaeol., X, Pt. 3: Fig. 28; also Pt. 4: 148, 155. See James B. Griffin, "Cultural Change and Continuity in Eastern United States Archaeology," Man in Northeastern North America, Papers of the R. S. Peabody Foundation for Archaeol., III: 37-95, Fig. 1.

[19]Cole and Deuel, op. cit., p. 222.

[20]Hoebel, op. cit., Pl. 14, specimens B and F, respectively.

[21]Eichenberger, op. cit., Pl. I, II, and X.

[22]M. R. Harrington, Certain Caddo Sites in Arkansas (New York: Heye Foundation, 1920). Note specimens g and k in Pl. CXV; b, c, e, f, and h in Pl. CXVI, and e in Pl. CXVII.

[23]Mr. Wilfred Logan was kind enough to make available and to discuss with me the materials he excavated at Graham Cave, Montgomery County, Missouri. In the bottom preceramic levels were points resembling No. 10 in blade type, concave base, and small lateral projections at the basal end of the blade edge. The points from Graham Cave, however, have deep side notches. Points similar to Nos. 4, 6, and 9 occur in the superimposed levels, associated with Woodland pottery. Reworking of points into drills and scrapers was also practiced at this site. Blades similar to No. 11 occur throughout the deposits.

cross dating, Webb and DeJarnette have worked out a projectile point chronology for the Pickwick Basin.[24] According to this chronology type No. 10 points are a marked characteristic of the preceramic horizon; they were introduced, reached their maximum, and became obsolete within what these authors call the Archaic 2 period.[25] Types like Nos. 6, 7, and 11 vary in importance in various periods, but are found throughout the series.

Point No. 5 is clearly like that of the Copena type.[26] Examination of the record of Copena sites $LU^{O}54$ and $LU^{V}65$ in the Pickwick Basin reveals that, in addition to the characteristic Copena points, the sites also yielded a few points of types Nos. 1, 7, 9, and 10 in addition to blades like No. 11.[27] These other points are not a constant feature of the sites, but they do provide some evidence of contemporaneity. Although type No. 10 disappears before the appearance of pottery in the Alabama shell mounds, a very few Copena-type points occur at prepottery levels.[28] It seems, therefore, that types Nos. 5 and 10 may occur together in the Pickwick area as they do at Cave Hollow. Such co-occurrence is either indicative of contemporaneity or of a disturbance of the original stratigraphy in both areas.

In Louisiana where the pottery affiliation is strong, Marksville stonework has no strong resemblances to that at Cave Hollow. Points like No. 6 occur at Marksville and in the top 6 inches at Tchefuncte. Troyville flintwork is practically unknown, but seems to resemble that of Marksville.[29]

[24]William S. Webb and David L. DeJarnette, *The Whitesburg Bridge Site Ma^{V} 10*, *Mus. Paper Ala. Mus. Nat. Hist.*, 24 (1948).

[25]*Ibid.*, p. 41. Cave Hollow point No. 10 appears to be equivalent to Pickwick types Nos. 30, 34, and 38.

[26]William S. Webb and David L. DeJarnette, *An Archaeological Survey of the Pickwick Basin in the Adjacent Portions of the State of Alabama, Mississippi and Tennessee*, *Bur. Amer. Ethnol. Bull.*, 129 (1942): Pl. 207.

[27]*Ibid.* Specimens similar to Cave Hollow types Nos. 1, 5, 7, and 11 illustrated in Plate 132 (2); types Nos. 5, 9, 10, and 11 in Plate 207 (2). A point similar to No. 4, except for its concave base, is also shown in Plate 207 (2).

[28]*Ibid.* The Copena type is Webb's type 37. See Plate 226 (2). Note occurrence of this type in Tables 24 and 32.

[29]Winslow M. Walker, *The Troyville Mounds, Catahoula Parish Louisiana*, *Bur. Amer. Ethnol. Bull.*, 113 (1936).

SUMMARY

The lowest levels of Cave Hollow represent a Bluff-Dweller occupation of the ceramic period. The presence of Baytown Plain ware places the site somewhere in the Marksville-Troyville-Coles Creek period. The occurrence of Mississippi ware in the top of the deposit indicates that occupation of the site probably lasted into the early Coles Creek epoch.

On the assumption that Cave Hollow parallels late Troyville and early Coles Creek, the stone material falls perfectly into the time period. The beginning of the Highland Aspect and late manifestation of the Boone Focus may well overlap in the middle Woodland of Missouri. This time period is parallel to that of middle Copena and late Hopewell.[30] The relatively short time span represented by the excavated deposit at Cave Hollow, in addition to the limited number of artifacts and lack of visible stratigraphy in the midden, makes it difficult to say whether the materials from the upper levels represent various transient groups or a single people experiencing wide contacts.

Cedar Grove Cave in Arkansas presented a similarly diverse collection of flintwork, but the stratigraphy was not discussed.[31] Whether Cave Hollow represents a single component or not, there is clear evidence that contact with or presence of Mississippi peoples occurred after the first habitation of the cave. The lack of other than pottery evidence of Mississippi culture may argue for contact rather than cultural succession. In view of the limited nature of the excavated deposit, it does not appear wise to make such an interpretation with finality. The temporal relationship of Cave Hollow to other prehistoric cultures does, however, seem to be established.

[30]Griffin, op. cit., Figs. 1 and 2.
[31]Walker, op. cit.

www.ingramcontent.com/pod-product-compliance
Lightning Source LLC
LaVergne TN
LVHW050022250826
846302LV00008B/67
* 9 7 8 1 9 4 9 0 9 8 4 0 2 *